WORLD'S FASTEST SPACECRAFT

APEX

By Hubert Walker

WWW.APEXEDITIONS.COM

Apex is distributed by North Star Editions:
sales@northstareditions.com | 888-417-0195

Produced for Apex by Red Line Editorial.

Photographs ©: Shutterstock Images, cover, 1, 6–7, 8; Bill Ingalls/NASA, 4–5; CSL, IAS, MPS, PMOD/WRC, ROB, UCL/MSSL/Solar Orbiter/EUI Team/ESA & NASA, 9; JSC/NASA, 10–11, 12, 16–17; MSFC/NASA, 13, 18–19, 20, 29; Art Directors & Trip/Alamy, 14–15; JPL-Caltech/NASA, 21; KSC/NASA, 22–23; JPL/NASA, 24–25; Johns Hopkins University Applied Physics Laboratory/Southwest Research Institute/JPL/NASA, 26, 27

Library of Congress Control Number: 2021918371

ISBN
978-1-63738-173-1 (hardcover)
978-1-63738-209-7 (paperback)
978-1-63738-277-6 (ebook pdf)
978-1-63738-245-5 (hosted ebook)

Printed in the United States of America
Mankato, MN
012022

NOTE TO PARENTS AND EDUCATORS

Apex books are designed to build literacy skills in striving readers. Exciting, high-interest content attracts and holds readers' attention. The text is carefully leveled to allow students to achieve success quickly. Additional features, such as bolded glossary words for difficult terms, help build comprehension.

TABLE OF CONTENTS

CHAPTER 1

PARKER SOLAR PROBE

Huge flames light up the night sky. A rocket blasts off. It is carrying the Parker Solar **Probe**.

The Parker Solar Probe lifted off on August 12, 2018.

This spacecraft studies the sun. The sun is a huge ball of flaming gas. So, the probe gets very hot as it speeds past.

Near the sun, the Parker Solar Probe faces temperatures much hotter than those inside a volcano.

DELTA IV HEAVY

The Delta IV Heavy is a large rocket. It sent the Parker Solar Probe into space. It is one of the most powerful rockets ever built.

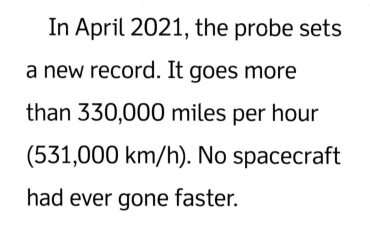

In April 2021, the probe sets a new record. It goes more than 330,000 miles per hour (531,000 km/h). No spacecraft had ever gone faster.

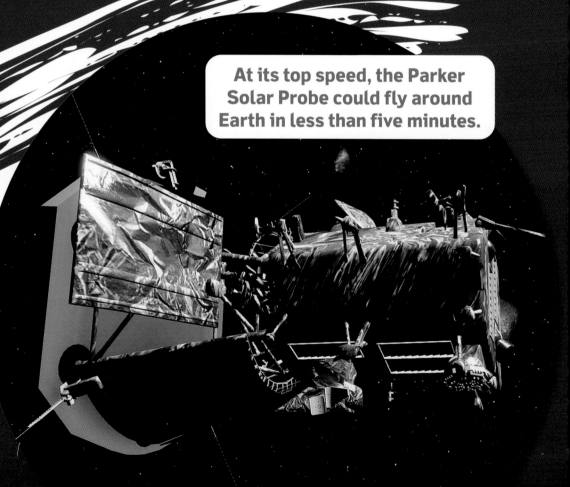

At its top speed, the Parker Solar Probe could fly around Earth in less than five minutes.

The Parker Solar Probe has flown closer to the sun than any other spacecraft.

Like many spacecraft, the Parker Solar Probe does not carry people.

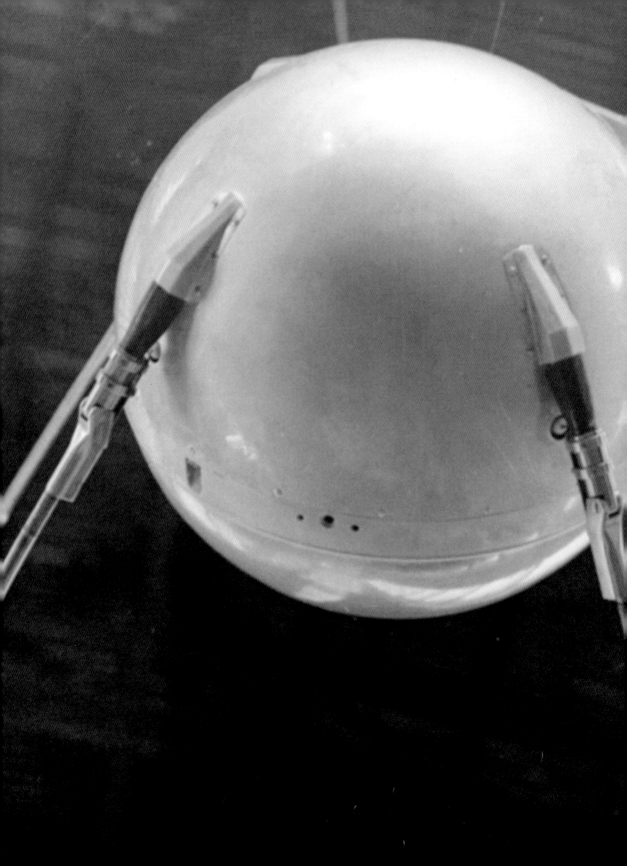

CHAPTER 2

HISTORY OF SPACECRAFT SPEED

The first spacecraft was called Sputnik 1. It traveled to space in 1957. It went 18,000 miles per hour (29,000 km/h).

Sputnik 1 was about the size of a beach ball. It circled Earth for three months.

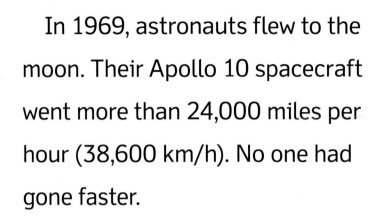

In 1969, astronauts flew to the moon. Their Apollo 10 spacecraft went more than 24,000 miles per hour (38,600 km/h). No one had gone faster.

Apollo 10 reached its top speed on its way back to Earth. The spacecraft landed in the Pacific Ocean in May 1969.

The Saturn V rocket stood 363 feet (111 m) tall.

SATURN V

Astronauts used the Saturn V rocket to reach the moon. It was the heaviest rocket ever made. It weighed 6.2 million pounds (2.8 million kg).

In the 1970s, scientists **launched** the Helios probes. These two spacecraft studied the sun. They reached speeds of more than 156,600 miles per hour (252,000 km/h).

The Helios probes are still moving around the sun today.

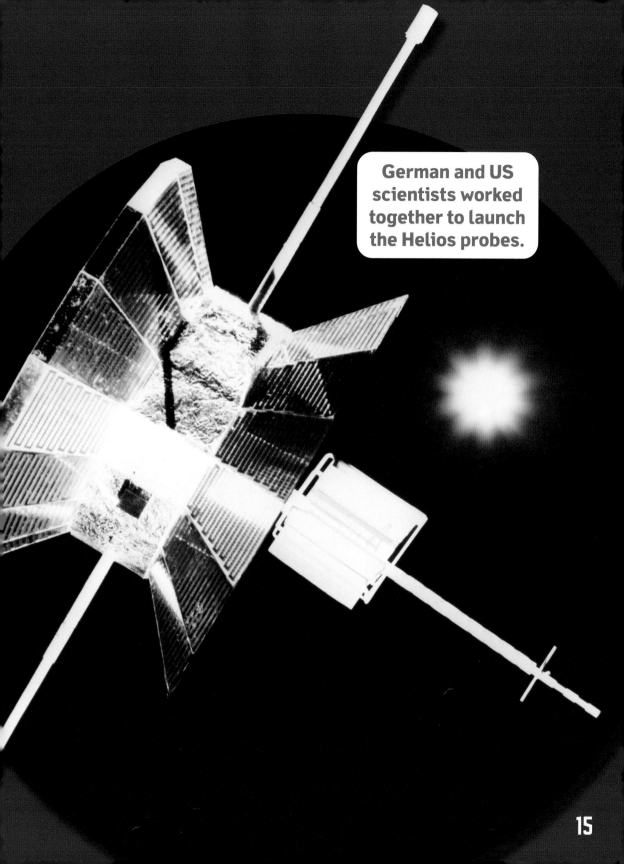

German and US scientists worked together to launch the Helios probes.

CHAPTER 3

ROCKET POWER

A rocket creates **thrust**. This force moves the spacecraft forward. To reach space, rockets must go very fast. They must be very powerful. And they need lots of **fuel**.

Space shuttles used about 2.2 million pounds (1 million kg) of fuel on each flight.

Rockets have **stages**. The first stage falls off after it uses up its fuel. Then the next stage starts using its own fuel.

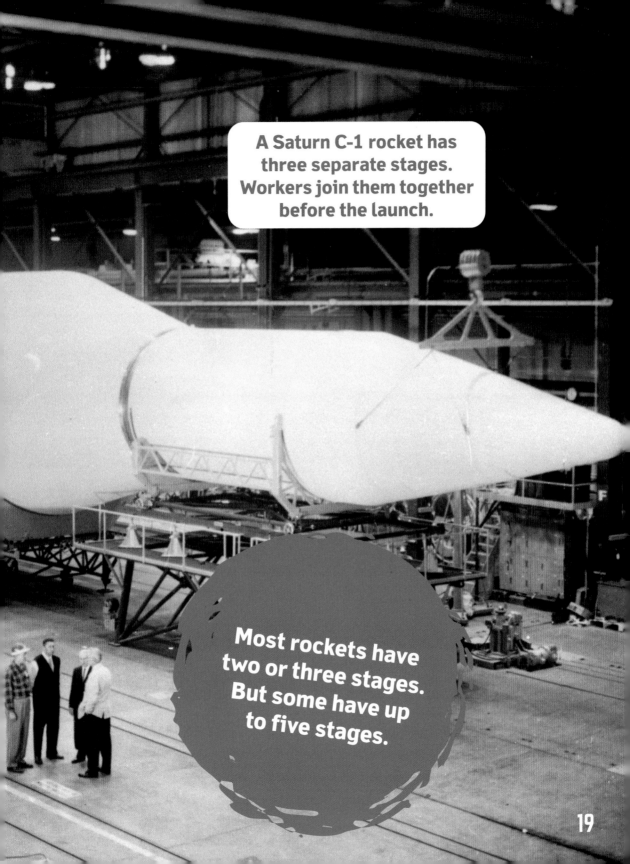

In 1977, scientists launched Voyager 1. This spacecraft used a Titan rocket. This rocket had three stages.

To reach space, rockets must go at least 17,000 miles per hour (27,000 km/h).

Voyager 1 has traveled farther than any other spacecraft.

VOYAGER 1

Voyager 1 went faster than 37,000 miles per hour (59,500 km/h). But it's still going. In 2012, it left the **solar system**. It entered **interstellar space**.

CHAPTER 4

USING GRAVITY

Rockets lift spacecraft into space. But before long, rockets run out of fuel. After that, spacecraft gain speed in other ways. Some use **gravity**.

Spacecraft are separated from rockets by the time they reach space.

Earth's solar system has eight planets. Every planet moves around the sun.

Planets have strong pulls because of gravity. They pull in smaller objects. So, a spacecraft goes faster when it flies past a planet.

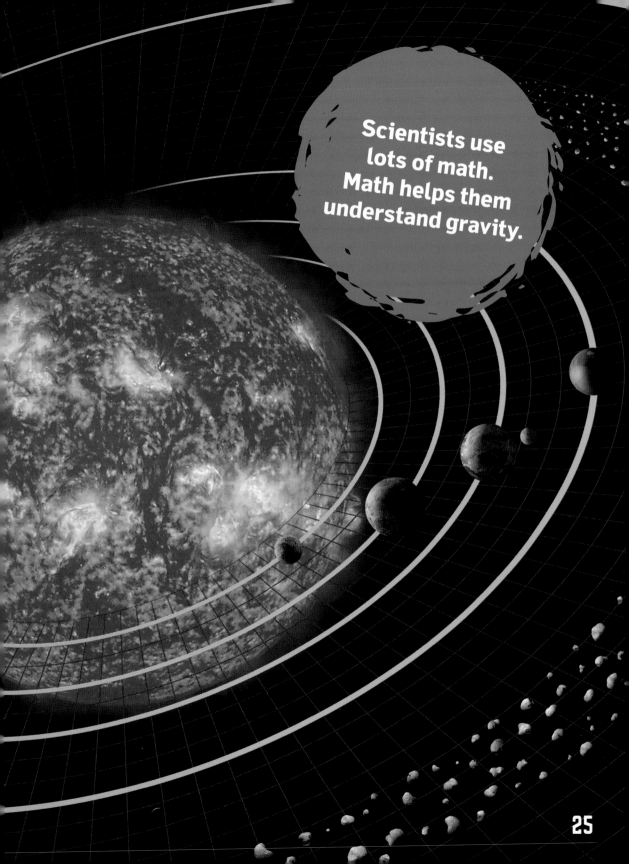

Scientists use lots of math. Math helps them understand gravity.

New Horizons used gravity. This spacecraft flew past Jupiter. It gained speed. Then it flew all the way to Pluto.

Passing Jupiter helped New Horizons go 9,000 miles per hour (14,500 km/h) faster.

New Horizons was launched in 2006.

New Horizons took
many pictures of Pluto.

SPEEDY SPACECRAFT

New Horizons was the first spacecraft to reach Pluto. It flew past Pluto in 2015. Then it kept going. At one point, it reached 33,000 miles per hour (53,000 km/h).

COMPREHENSION QUESTIONS

Write your answers on a separate piece of paper.

1. Write a sentence that explains the main ideas of Chapter 3.

2. Would you like to travel in a spacecraft? Why or why not?

3. What was the name of the first spacecraft?

    A. Parker Solar Probe

    B. Voyager 1

    C. Sputnik 1

4. What might happen if a rocket did not have stages?

    A. It might give a spacecraft too much thrust.

    B. It might not have enough power to leave Earth.

    C. It might go much faster than a rocket with stages.

5. What does **record** mean in this book?

*In April 2021, the probe sets a new **record**. It goes more than 330,000 miles per hour (531,000 km/h). No spacecraft had ever gone faster.*

    A. something that is worse than all others
    B. something that is faster than all others
    C. something that is older than all others

6. What does **astronauts** mean in this book?

*In 1969, **astronauts** flew to the moon. Their Apollo 10 spacecraft went more than 24,000 miles per hour (38,600 km/h).*

    A. people who drive cars
    B. people who travel in space
    C. people who build spacecraft

Answer key on page 32.

GLOSSARY

fuel
Something that can make power when it is burned.

gravity
A force that pulls objects toward planets, stars, and other huge objects.

interstellar space
The parts of space outside the strong pulls of stars.

launched
Sent something into space.

planets
Large objects in space that move around the sun.

probe
A type of spacecraft that gathers information.

solar system
An area that includes the sun and all of the planets and other objects that move around it.

stages
Parts of a rocket that give it power.

thrust
A force that pushes something in a certain direction.

TO LEARN MORE

BOOKS

Hutchison, Patricia. *Race to Space*. Mankato, MN: The Child's World, 2019.

Klepeis, Alicia Z. *Superfast Rockets*. Minneapolis: Jump!, 2022.

Mara, Wil. *Breakthroughs in Space Travel*. Minneapolis: Lerner Publications, 2019.

ONLINE RESOURCES

Visit **www.apexeditions.com** to find links and resources related to this title.

ABOUT THE AUTHOR

Hubert Walker enjoys running, hunting, and going to the dog park with his best pal. He grew up in Georgia but moved to Minnesota in 2018. Overall, he loves his new home, but he's not a fan of the cold winters.

INDEX

Answer Key:
1. Answers will vary; 2. Answers will vary; 3. C; 4. B; 5. B; 6. B